Quotable Tiger

Quotable Tiger

A Grand Slam Compendium of Compelling Quotes
by and about TIGER WOODS,
Golf Champion Extraordinaire

Rich Skyzinski

TowleHouse Publishing
Nashville, Tennessee

TowleHouse books are distributed by National Book Network (NBN), 4720 Boston Way, Lanham, Maryland 20706.

Cataloging-in-Publication data is available.
ISBN: 1-931249-00-8

Cover design by Gore Studio, Inc.
Page design by Mike Towle

Printed in the United States of America
1 2 3 4 5 6 — 05 04 03 02 01

Contents

Acknowledgments

I WISH TO THANK Maxine Vigliotta and Tanya Gray in the photo archive department at the United States Golf Association; the reference desk at the Fort Myers (Florida) and Lee County Public Library; and Marty Parkes and the Communications Department at the United States Golf Association. A special thanks goes to my wife, Susan, whose invaluable research skills made this book possible.

Introduction

W HEN HE WON the 1997 Masters by a laughable twelve-stroke margin, Tiger Woods did more than lap the field. It was as though he had grabbed the collective golf world by the lapels and slammed it up against the wall, getting our rapt attention.

Overnight he became the single most important drawing card sought by every tournament director, and when galleries turned out in record numbers because of his presence, so did the hordes of writers and broadcasters, each one desperate to get a one-on-one interview with Tiger. Whatever Woods had to say was priority number one for the newshounds. Who won the tournament was secondary.

Other golfers who had come along before Woods had also been media darlings, and some won frequently as well, but it wasn't long before Woods became, without question, the most quoted golfer in history. It quickly became customary procedure to bring Woods into the press room for a pretournament interview—every time he played. And with his prodigious talents securing his place at or near the top of the leader board, it wasn't unusual for Woods to do five press conferences in a single week—one on the Tuesday or Wednesday prior to the start of the event, then one on each of the four days after he'd concluded his round.

It also got to the point where Woods was included on the list of pretournament interviews for each and every PGA Tour event in which he was entered, a practice Woods felt was a matter of overkill. No other player was asked to sit down in front of a podium of microphones as often, Woods argued, a point of questionable merit when one compares his star appeal with anyone else in the field. But after discussions with PGA Tour officials, a compromise of sorts was agreed upon; majors aside, Woods would conduct a pre-tournament press conference only at those events in which he was defending champion or playing for the first time.

Hogan, Palmer, and Nicklaus were all headliners—the best of their respective eras—but none possessed the drawing power of Woods, who, it can be argued, may single-handedly be responsible for golf's growing appeal worldwide. Examples have been strewn from Dublin to Denver, from Boston to Bangkok. Woods plays, and resultant ticket sales reach unprecedented numbers. The size of press rooms doubles. Is it mere coincidence that the highest-rated Masters, U.S. Open, British Open, and PGA Championship telecasts in history have all involved a Woods victory?

Even more confounding is that viewers aren't tuning in for the competition. Many are watching simply to see Woods, much like starstruck movie buffs who will run out to see a Tom Cruise movie even if they don't understand the plot. "My children were riveted to the television set," former U.S. Senate candidate Ronna Romney told CNN in an interview after Woods's historic 1997 Masters win. "I can't stand golf on television. I think it's the most boring thing in the world. I was riveted."

Amateur golf has never attracted a larger television audience than the pros, but it did in 1996 when Woods won his third consecutive U.S. Amateur title. In a head-to-head match against the PGA Tour's simultaneously telecast World Series of Golf, Woods's final match against Steve Scott, a dramatic battle that went to a sudden-death playoff, outdrew the pros . . . rather sizably at that.

"What we've found in covering any PGA Tour event," an NBC spokesman told *Sports Illustrated*, "is that if Tiger's on the Sunday leader board, that's worth an extra one and a half Nielsen points or more. That's huge."

Of course, the emergence of such a world-renowned superstar does not come without its share of hiccups. Woods's father, Earl, has occasionally spoken both too freely and too brashly, proclaiming golf as merely the vehicle through which Tiger fulfills his greater purpose in life. In his profanity-laced article in GQ, Charles P. Pierce responded to Earl's conviction that the second coming of the Messiah wears a Nike swoosh and fist-pumps his way across the landscape after belting three-hundred-yard drives and making long putts that win golf tournaments. Wrote Pierce: "I do not believe—right now, this day—that Tiger Woods will change humanity any more than Chuck Berry did."

Whether the controversial story in GQ, which included off-color jokes told by Woods, was done with Woods's understanding that his comments were on the record or not, his statements have on more than a few occasions irritated his fellow PGA Tour brethren. Perhaps none caused a larger uproar than his claim in May 1997, when he said his play during the final round of the Byron Nelson Classic, which he won, was, in his estimation, no better than a C-plus performance. Truth be told, he was coaxed into that response by a writer following up on a grading estimate Woods had casually given in passing a few days earlier.

"He didn't want to give himself a grade," remembers *Dallas Morning News* golf writer Brad Townsend. "But the writer wouldn't give up."

But whatever media and gallery attention Woods commands is completely deserved. Many believe he merits comparison with the game's greats not only because of the rate at which he wins, but because his many talents are the best the game has ever seen. The stories of Woods's prodigious length are legendary, but he is hardly one-dimensional. His short game is impeccable. Others feel he's made the most noticeable improvement in his putting. And his creativity, his confidence, his flair for the dramatic . . . has there ever been a more complete package?

When he was only seventeen, Woods made a stirring comeback to capture a record third straight U.S. Junior Amateur title. In the final match at Waverley Country Club in Portland, Oregon, he was 2 down with two holes to play, then birdied the seventeenth and eighteenth holes to force extra holes, before he went on to win at the nineteenth.

When asked how he managed to birdie the last two holes of regulation, seemingly because he willed it so, he answered that he did it "because I had to. I had no other choice."

That explanation, while simplistic, is also part hyperbole, embellishment, and exaggeration. No player can make a birdie simply because he wants to. The game's harder than that. Even for Tiger Woods.

Quotable
Tiger

ADVICE

My dad once told me, "No matter what anyone says or writes, really, none of those people
have to hit your little four-foot putt . . . You
have to go do it yourself."

Just be yourself.
—*referring to the best advice he'd ever received from his parents*

AMBITIONS AND GOALS

There's nothing wrong with having your goals really high and trying to achieve them.[1]

~

What drives me is to become more consistent, to try to get better.[2]

~

WHAT IMPRESSES ME THE MOST ABOUT HIM IS THE FACT THAT, AS GOOD AS HE IS AS THE GOLFER WHO'S CONSIDERED THE BEST PLAYER IN THE WORLD, AND MAYBE THE BEST EVER, HE'S STILL NOT SATISFIED. FOR ALL HIS WEALTH, HE STILL HAS THE DRIVE, HE STILL HAS THE DESIRE TO PLAY GOLF AS WELL AS HE CAN. I JUST ADMIRE THE WAY HE CARRIES HIM-SELF, BUT IN A WAY, I FEEL SORRY FOR HIM. BACK WHEN I PLAYED WELL, I HAD ABOUT ONE-THOUSANDTH OF THE ATTENTION HE'S GETTING.

—Byron Nelson

~

Daddy, do you think when I turn pro you could live off $100,000 a year?[3]

—*at age ten*

⌒

If it (golf) is your lifelong passion, you can't imagine not being part of it. I might be like Arnie, play until I'm seventy.[4]

⌒

I can tell you one thing. This is something I've said and will continue to say. I'm going to try to get better.
—*at the 2000 U.S. Open, when asked about his greatness*

⌒

UNTIL TIGER WOODS LOSES HIS GIFTS, WHICH COULD TAKE TWENTY YEARS OR MORE, NOT TOO MANY AMBITIOUS YOUNG MEN ARE GOING TO AWAKEN EVERY MORNING WITH THE DREAM OF BEING THE BEST GOLFER WHO EVER LIVED. THAT JOB'S TAKEN.[5]

—*Thomas Boswell, columnist*

⌒

Just get the *W* and go home.[6]

I always say that I don't care what anyone says, whether it's the media, family, friends, or anybody else. I know what I want to do, and I'm going to go out there and try and do it.[7]

TIGER PAUSE

Since 1950, only two players—Arnold Palmer in 1960 and Johnny Miller in 1974—have won as many as eight times on the PGA Tour. Woods did it in both 1999 and 2000.

I know what I want to accomplish, and I know how to get there.[8]

The ultimate goal is to be the best. Whether that's the best ever, who knows? I hope so. What I truly hope is that the best I can be will be good enough to become that.[9]

⌒

That's not the way I am. I've always been a person who does anything to win.
—on Larry King Live *in 1998, talking about the possibility of becoming complacent over the increased prize money in golf instead of winning*

⌒

You always want to put yourself in a position where you are not going to beat yourself. They are going to have to beat you.

⌒

There's nothing wrong with having your goals very high and trying to get to them. That's the fun part. You may come up short. I've come up short on a lot on my goals, but it's always fun to try and achieve them.

⌒

I just want to win golf tournaments. That's all I want to do. That's what I get my big kick out of. And just having the chance to win a golf tournament . . . coming down the stretch, that adrenaline flowing, you have a chance, you really do have a chance, and that's such a great feeling.

For me, my priorities are obviously to win the big ones. And the big ones are the majors . . . That is how someone will be remembered.

I don't think you're ever finished. As soon as you feel like you're finished, then I guess you are finished, because you've already put a limit on your ability and what you can attain.

—responding to 1999 query about how close his swing was to being finished

TIGER PAUSE

Woods was the first PGA Tour player to surpass each million-dollar mark, from $2 million to $9 million, in single-season earnings.

If I show up at a tournament, my number-one goal is just to win, do whatever it takes to accomplish that.

I really don't believe that there is such a thing as perfection because we are human. We are all technically imperfect, so how can we ever achieve perfection? But what I will tell you is this: That I have always been a big believer of professional excellence, and that is what I try and achieve. I know I can never get to a point where I hit perfect shots every time.

When I turned pro I felt I would contend in a number of major championships.

>*—at the 2000 British Open, about to win the second of his three 2000 major victories*

Woods had this response at the 1998 Masters when asked, "If God came down and said, 'Tiger, you can win only one major this year,' which major would it be?":

The way I am, I'd argue with Him and say, "Why can't I have all four?"

It's not like saying, "Well, it would be a great week if he could make the cut." I think if my game ever got to that, it wouldn't be a good thing. But if they expect me to win every week, that means I'm right there a lot and I have a chance.

TIGER PAUSE

Before Woods turned twenty-five, he became the PGA Tour's all-time leading money-winner.

AUGUSTA

This is crazy. I never thought it would ever be like this in my entire life.[10]

—after his 1997 Masters triumph

They're changing the golf course and the way it's meant to be played. I'm going to have to play a little more of a different game. This golf course is not set up where the winning score is going to be a real low score like in the past.

—at the 2000 Masters

I guess that's something they like to do around this place. I don't know. Maybe they get bored.[11]

—about changes to Augusta National Golf Club

Well, I did shoot 40 on my first nine holes.

—when asked if he could have done better after winning in 1997 by twelve strokes

At Augusta, a lot of it is luck. You are going to hit some shots in there that are borderline, going to catch the slope and feed down to the hole. You are going to make about a ten-footer for birdie when you should be chipping for . . . a par and probably make bogey. These are the things that you need to have happen.

～

I first realized the magnitude once I got back here: was playing golf yesterday . . . all by myself. It's seven o'clock, and there are about a thousand people out there following you on a Monday afternoon, screaming my name, wanting me to look this way, look that way, look this way, look that way, for a picture. That wasn't the case last year. I played nine holes in absolute solitude last year.

—*at Augusta in 1998, the year after his incredible victory there*

～

I think the greatest thing I did there was not drive the ball, because I can hit the ball that length any day. It's the way I putted. . . .To go around that golf course and never have a three-putt, I think, was more of an accomplishment than anything else.

—on his 1997 Masters triumph

I forgive, but I don't forget.[12]

—discussing Fuzzy Zoeller's offensive remarks about "collard greens," etc., at the 1997 Masters

Everything here is so perfect. I get to live here, they serve us great food, and all I have to do is walk out the door to use the best practice facility and the best course in the world. How can you not play well?[13]

Your tournament will always hold a special spot in my heart as the place where I made my first PGA cut and at a major yet! It is here that I have left my youth behind and became a man. For that I will be eternally in your debt.[14]

—excerpt from letter Woods wrote to Augusta National officials in 1996, while still an amateur

CAREER (SO FAR)

This is to confirm that, as of now, I am a professional golfer.

—*Milwaukee Open press conference, August 1996*

WOODS IS THE MOST AMAZING PERFORMER I'VE EVER SEEN, AND I'VE SEEN ALI, GRETZKY, JORDAN, MONTANA, AND NICKLAUS. WHAT WOODS IS DOING IS SO HARD IT'S LIKE CLIMBING EVEREST IN FLIP-FLOPS. PERFORMING HEART TRANSPLANTS IN OVEN MITTS.[15]

—*Rick Reilly, columnist*

TIGER PAUSE

In 2000, Woods was a cumulative fifty-three under par in the four professional majors, the best mark in history by a whopping twenty-five strokes. Nick Faldo, twenty-eight under in 1990, is second.

THE CLOSEST THING TO TIGER WOODS IN RECENT DECADES
HAS BEEN SECRETARIAT BARRELING THROUGH THE 1973
TRIPLE CROWN, WINNING THE BELMONT BY THIRTY-ONE
LENGTHS, SO FAR AHEAD THAT THE OTHER HORSES COULD
ONLY SURMISE BY HIS HOOFPRINTS THAT THEY WERE INDEED
IN A RACE.[16]

—*George Vescey, sports columnist*

It's a weird feeling because you know stepping up over
a golf shot that you can shape the ball the way you
want to with the right trajectory and land the ball on
what number you want. If you have 163 . . . you land
the ball (on) 163 . . . not 164, not 162; it's right on
the number. It's a feeling, if you're lucky, you probably
get maybe a handful of times in your entire lifetime.

TIGER PAUSE

Woods first reached No. 1 in the world rankings when he was only twenty-one years old.

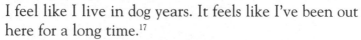

I feel like I live in dog years. It feels like I've been out here for a long time.[17]

—*spoken in 2000, his fifth year as a pro and right after he had won the World Series of Golf by eleven shots with a 259 total*

HE'S THE MOST DOMINANT GOLFER WHO EVER LIVED.[18]

—*Gary Player*

Those are true champions right there. Everyone is a true champion; they have won numerous, countless tournaments, really. They've been the cream of the crop. They've been the elite players . . . to ever play the game. And to be in the same breath as those guys it makes it very special, very special.

—*in July 2000, talking about other British Open champions*

I've played better before in my life, but I've never been in this circumstance where I've played this good.

—*after his third straight U.S. Amateur victory (1996)*

TIGER PAUSE

Having won twenty matches against two defeats, Woods's career winning percentage in the match play portion of the U.S. Amateur is .909. Second on the list among players with a minimum of twenty career victories is Bobby Jones at .843.

THE BETTER YOU PLAY, THE BETTER IT'S MAKING ME LOOK. SO KEEP ON GOING.[19]

—*Darren Clarke, Irish golfer who beat Woods in the final of the Andersen Consulting Match Play Championship*

ARNOLD AND I BOTH AGREED YOU COULD TAKE ALL
HIS MASTERS AND ALL MINE, AND TIGER COULD
WIN MORE THAN BOTH OF US PUT TOGETHER
BEFORE HE'S DONE.

—*Jack Nicklaus, at the 1996 Masters,*
when Woods was still an amateur

IT'S REVOLUTIONARY RATHER THAN EVOLUTIONARY
CHANGE. HE REMINDS ME OF MICHAEL JORDAN
MORE THAN ANYONE I'VE SEEN. HE DOESN'T
BROOD OVER MISTAKES, HE LEARNS FROM THEM.[20]

—*Dr. Richard Coop, renowned sports psychologist,*
referring to Woods's talent level

CHILDHOOD

I did the same things every kid did. I studied and went
to the mall. I was addicted to TV wrestling, rap music,
and *The Simpsons*. I got into trouble and got out of it. I
loved my parents and obeyed what they told me. The
only difference is I can sometimes hit a little ball into
a hole in less (sic) strokes than some other people.[21]

OTHER GUYS HAVE BEEN WORRIED ABOUT HIM SINCE HE WAS
EIGHT YEARS OLD. PARENTS USED TO CALL THE HOUSE AND
ASK, "IS TIGER PLAYING NEXT WEEK?
    "OH, HE'S NOT?
    "WELL, THEN, I THINK MY SON'S GOING TO PLAY."[22]

—*Earl Woods, Tiger's dad*

TIGER PAUSE

Woods won three United States Junior
Amateurs (1991–93). No player has ever won
more than once, and only four players have
played in the final match twice.

I learned my pop's phone number at work when I was two years old. I would call and ask him if I could go practice with him. He always said yes.[23]

TIGER PAUSE

Competing against ten- and eleven-year-olds, Woods won a Pitch, Putt, and Drive competition—when he was three.

Don't force your kids into sports. I never was. To this day, my dad has never asked me to go play golf. I ask him. It's the child's desire to play that matters, not the parent's desire to have the child play. Keep it fun.[24]

There's more to life than golf. I've always had to finish my homework before playing.[25]

MY PRIMARY CONCERN WAS TO RAISE A GOOD PERSON. ATH-
LETIC ACHIEVEMENTS WERE SECONDARY.[26]

—*Earl Woods*

HE WAS THE BEST FIFTEEN-YEAR-OLD PLAYER I HAD EVER
SEEN. HE WAS THE BEST AT SIXTEEN AND SEVENTEEN AND SO
ON. HE'S THE BEST TWENTY-ONE-YEAR-OLD PLAYER ANYONE
HAS EVER SEEN. I'M EXCITED TO SEE HOW GOOD HE'S GOING
TO BE WHEN HE'S TWENTY-TWO. IF HE KEEPS GETTING BET-
TER, OH BOY. I'M NOT SURE GOLF HAS SEEN ANYTHING LIKE
HIM BEFORE. MAYBE BOBBY JONES.[27]

—*Byron Nelson*

When you fly (from the) west, you always lose time.
That's tough on your body, especially on a sixteen-
year-old body, and I'm sick of that.[28]

HIS CLUBS

All fourteen are my favorites. If they are not my favorites, they are not in the bag.

—when asked what his favorite club was

All of them.

—when asked what iron he has the most confidence in

Tiger in 1991, en route to winning the first of his three U.S. Junior Amateur titles (USGA photo by Rick Dole)

COLLEGE

Education always has been my first priority. That's why I chose Stanford. Golf is secondary. Even if I win three (U.S.) Amateur titles, I'll stay in school to get my degree in business.[29]

⌒

Dad, remember how I had a slight overbite? Well, my teeth are lined up perfect now.[30]

> —*recalling part of a conversation he had with his father after he was mugged on the Stanford campus*

⌒

COLOR OF SKIN

There are still courses in the U.S. I am not allowed to play because of the color of my skin. Hello world. I've heard I'm not ready for you. Are you ready for me?

—his lines in a Nike commercial he made soon after turning pro in 1996

~

THIS COULD BE AS SIGNIFICANT AS JACKIE ROBINSON'S BREAKTHROUGH IN BASEBALL FIFTY YEARS AGO, BECAUSE NOW WE'LL NEVER HAVE A SITUATION AGAIN WHERE PEOPLE WILL TURN THEIR HEADS WHEN A BLACK MAN WALKS ON THE FIRST TEE AT A COUNTRY CLUB.

—Lee Elder, the first African-American ever to play in the Masters, watching Woods win at Augusta in 1997

~

They don't like me at my home course (the Navy Golf Club, Cypress, California). They try to shut me out. I think it's my skin color. My dad outranks them all, and he happens to have a son who plays golf. The pro let me play when I was four, but all the members got mad because I was beating them.[31]

—at age fifteen

TIGER PAUSE

Woods broke 50 for nine holes for the first time when he was just three years old, playing at the Navy Golf Club in Cypress, California.

COOL DUDE

Thanks, stud.[32]

>   —to Davis Love III, his playoff opponent in the
>   1996 Las Vegas Invitational, in response to
>   Love's congratulations to Woods for playing so well.
>   Woods then defeated Love for his first PGA Tour victory.

Maybe I should run up through there like it's a tunnel at a football game and explode onto the tee box and high-five everybody.[33]

When people yell, "You're the man," I always say, "Not legally."[34]

>   —in 1996, soon after turning pro several
>   months shy of his twenty-first birthday

THE HARDEST PART IS LISTENING TO THAT GAWD-
AWFUL MUSIC HE LISTENS TO.[35]

> —*Butch Harmon, Woods's instructor, talking about what
> it's like to be a passenger in Woods's car*

The way I feel about my game, I just might
blow everybody away this week.

> —*spoken right before he won the
> 2000 U.S. Open by fifteen shots*

FAMILY

Their teachings assist me in almost every decision I make. They are my foundation.[36]

~

Pop is my best friend.[37]

~

There are three things that I really care about. My family, playing tournament golf, and working with and helping young kids.[38]

~

FANS AND GALLERIES

I've played an Eisenhower Cup, which is like the World Amateur, in France; a Walker Cup in Wales; a Ryder Cup in Spain; Presidents Cup in Australia. I've never played here. So, it's nice to go out there and play and have some fans cheering for us and some good shots and I don't have to hear boos all day.

—*at the 1999 Ryder Cup, in Brookline, Massachusetts*

I really don't know if I'm giving them thrills or not, I'm just trying to make golf shots and give myself a chance to win.

—*about fulfilling the expectations of the gallery*

HE STILL LEADS THE WORLD IN POLICE ESCORTS GOING FROM TEE TO GREEN AND WALKING TO THE CLUBHOUSE EVERY DAY.[39]

—*John Feinstein*

HE CAN'T GO MANY PLACES WITHOUT BEING MOBBED LIKE A
ROCK STAR.[40]

—golf writer Pete McDaniel

That's why I'm here and you're over there.
*—at the 1998 Doral Ryder Open, explaining why he didn't hit
driver off the tee as fans implored him to*

TIGER TOOK A WOOD OUT OF HIS BAG.
    THE GALLERY ERUPTED.
    IT HAS BEEN A LONG TIME SINCE ANY GOLF GALLERY
CHEERED SOMEONE FOR REMOVING A CLUB FROM HIS BAG.
THE OVATION WAS NOT ABOUT REDEMPTION OR ABOUT INSPI-
RATION. IT WAS NOT ABOUT THE METAPHYSICAL MAUNDER-
ING OF THEOLOGICAL DILETTANTES. IT WAS ABOUT COURAGE
AND RISK AND ATHLETIC DARING.[41]

—Charles P. Pierce, writing in GQ magazine

FOOD

There's a difference between here and the States, but not much. The portions aren't as big. I order a super-size fries and get about as many as I get in a large in the States. The food isn't as greasy, either, and I really love the grease. Just about wherever I go, if there's McDonald's there, I'll find it.[42]

—while in England for the 1996 British Open at Royal Lytham and St. Annes, where a nearby Burger King and two McDonald's beckoned

THE GAME

I am just like you guys. I'm a human being, and all I do is chase a little white ball around.[43]

~

When I was young, it wasn't cool to play golf. And there certainly wasn't anything cool to wear to play golf. I love it. It's all changing around.[44]

~

GOLF IS A GAME WHERE YOU MATURE LATE, MOST OF THE TIME. MOST GREAT CHAMPIONS, JACK NICKLAUS BEING THE MOST OBVIOUS EXCEPTION, DON'T START WINNING MAJOR TITLES TILL LATE IN THEIR TWENTIES, EVEN INTO THEIR THIR-TIES. AND WHEN THIS KID COMES ALONG, TWENTY-ONE YEARS OLD, A COLLEGE DROPOUT EIGHT MONTHS AGO, AND IS BEATING YOUR BRAINS IN, IT DOES PSYCH YOU OUT.[45]

—John Feinstein

~

A lot of times you are not always going to outplay everybody. You are going to have to have some help sometimes.

We definitely hit the ball farther than most, but to be honest with you, in fifteen years from now we're not going to be the longest hitters anymore. There are going to be kids that are going to be longer and stronger than us.

Any time you ever play a tournament when you can play lift, clean, and cheat . . . it's imperative you drive the ball to the fairway. Because it's a huge advantage to . . . get the lie you want, every hole out there.

I CAN'T IMAGINE ANY COURSE THAT DOESN'T FAVOR TIGER.
IT DOESN'T MATTER WHAT COURSE YOU PUT HIM ON, HE'LL
PLAY WELL.[46]

—Jack Nicklaus

To be honest, I could(n't) care less. I've always
believed once you're at a tournament site, then your
reign is over. You're a champion of the tournament for
fifty-one weeks. When the week comes around, the
tournament is up for grabs.

—at 2000 Memorial Tournament,
preparing to defend his 1999 title there

HE IS AN INCREDIBLE MAN THAT'S PLAYED GOLF LIKE
NOBODY IN THE UNIVERSE HAS EVER PLAYED. MAYBE OUT
THERE IN SOME OTHER UNIVERSE SOME GUY CAN DO THIS.
BUT IN THIS ONE, WHERE WE ARE, NOBODY HAS EVER
STEPPED INTO A PAIR OF GOLF SHOES AND PLAYED THE GAME
LIKE HE HAS.

—Grant Waite, PGA Tour golfer, defeated by
Woods at the 2000 Canadian Open

TIGER PAUSE

Woods's long-hitting rivalry with John Daly actually dates all the way back to the late eighties, when fate brought them together as partners in the Insurance Golf Classic, which had a junior-pro format that brought the thirteen-year-old Woods and Daly together in 1989.[47]

I've paid my dues. I've worked really hard. And again, I've been really lucky, too. I've had some good breaks and some good things in my life go the right way. And it could have easily gone the other way. But I've had some good things happen in my life and I've been very fortunate.

Golf humbles you every day, every shot, really. I know how hard the game is.[48]

You play for . . . three and a half days. You give yourself a chance on the back nine on Sunday, with everything on the line. I think that's why we all get out there and try to compete.

⌒

I could be the greatest range player of all time out there, but if I do it on the golf course down the stretch, that's a big difference.

⌒

The eye of the Tiger, lining up a putt at the 1994 U.S. Amateur. (USGA photo by Robert Walker)

What I did last week
doesn't really matter
this week.

There are times when you hit a shot and you pull it off. To be able to pull off some certain shots that . . . you look back in hindsight and you wonder, How did I do that? It felt so easy at the time. You drop the same ball there with nobody around and you try to do it again, it would be a lot harder to do.

I love playing golf more than I ever have, and I thought that was impossible. I can't wait to get out there. As soon as I make it to the range, it's like, ahhhhh . . . Peace at last.[49]

I think I will continue to learn how to play this game until the day I die. It always changes. You always will learn. That's one of the great things about it.

I've got beaten by people that I thought I should never get beaten by, and I've beat people that I thought should never have been beaten by me. That's one of the beauties of match play and that's why we all love to play.

⌒

You can't win every time you're in the hunt. Unfortunately, we would like to. But it just doesn't happen that way. The key is to keep giving yourself chances.

⌒

You're going to go through some periods where you're just not at the top of your game. That doesn't mean that you're going to stay there; that just means that just like anything, it comes in cycles, and you've got to ride the highs when you're there and get through the lows as quick as possible.

⌒

Anybody can beat anybody. That's the problem with match play. Then again, that's the beauty of it.[50]

⌒

There are two opponents in the game, yourself and the golf course. If you can somehow combat those two, you'll do all right.[51]

⌒

Woods digging his game out of the ground in the third round of the 1999 U.S. Open. (USGA photo by J. D. Cuban).

You can never master the game. Simple as that.[52]

~

TIGER PAUSE

In 2000 Woods played forty-seven consecutive rounds in PGA Tour events in par or better, a record he improved by more than 50 percent. For the year, he played seventy-six rounds and was over par in only six.

~

It's one of the only games in which you can go out
there and play your absolute best and still not shoot as
good a score as when you played horrible.[53]

Even when I was a little boy playing junior golf, I have
always loved playing the hardest golf courses because I
think that is when it is the most challenging. I don't
enjoy having to go out there and have to shoot mid-
twenties (under par) in order to win. That, to me, is
just not fun. It is not the challenge that I like. I like to
go out there and grind away and knowing that par is a
good score . . . Most tournaments now you shoot that
and you get passed.

HEROES

There's no doubt that I arrived at the right time. When you look at the accomplishments of a Lee Elder or Charlie Sifford, you realize that if I had come along in the sixties or seventies I wouldn't have had a chance. Those guys have knocked down the doors for me to play. And I plan to take full advantage of it.[54]

WHEN I TELL (MY CHILDREN) THAT DAMN NEAR EVERY KID IN THE WORLD ONCE WANTED TO BE LIKE AN ATHLETE NAMED MICHAEL JORDAN, AND NOT TIGER WOODS, THEY'LL PROBABLY LOOK AT EACH OTHER AND SAY, "MICHAEL WHO?"[55]

—*Roy S. Johnson, journalist*

WOODS IS A GOLFER, AND WITHOUT DOUBT THE BEST YOUNG GOLFER IN THE COUNTRY, AN ATHLETE WHOSE SUCCESSES ARE SO SPECTACULAR AS TO SUGGEST MORE THE IMPROBABLE EXPLOITS OF A SPORTS-FICTION HERO THAN A CREATURE OF REAL LIFE.

—Robert Seigel, National Public Radio commentator

I got in last night and I got the pro-am pairing sheet, and there is my name at nine o'clock and there is an open space right behind me. That was a rude awakening. You almost think it was a dream, a bad dream, or a nightmare, but unfortunately, it came true.

—at the 1999 Tour Championship,
talking about Payne Stewart's death

I'm definitely not a pioneer. That's for people like Jackie Robinson and Lee Elder. I'm just a product of their hard work.[56]

—after winning the 1997 Masters

TIGER PAUSE

One of Woods's nongolfing heroes, or at least influences, was figure skater Debi Thomas, an African-American who won a medal at the 1988 Winter Olympics and attended Stanford. Woods was only twelve when, he said, he first took an interest in Stanford academics while watching Thomas skate.[57]

HUMOR

Is sleeping a sport?[58]

> —*in response to a question as to whether he intended to play another sport*

I'm asking for strokes now.

> —*when asked what difference his buddy Mark O'Meara's 1998 Masters win had made in their relationship*

On my golf course it would be about seven to eight hundred yards.

> —*discussing the length of par-fours and par-fives he'd build if he were a golf course architect*

The best year of my life was when I was eleven. I got straight A's, had two recesses a day, and the cutest girlfriend, and won thirty-two tournaments that year. Everything's been downhill since.[59]

IMPACT ON THE GAME

Now kids will think golf is cool.[60]

—after winning the 1997 Masters

⌒

HE'S A LEGEND IN THE MAKING. HE'S TWENTY-FOUR. HE'S PROBABLY GOING TO BE BIGGER THAN ELVIS WHEN HE GETS INTO HIS FORTIES.

—Ernie Els, January 2000

⌒

It bothered me when I was younger because I was the only one of any minority playing golf. Now I'm starting to see more minority faces in the crowd. And it's cool to see these people taking a serious interest in golf. My goal from the outset was to make golf look like America. Hopefully, when I am finished with golf or six feet under, I can leave the game better than it was when I entered.[61]

⌒

I think I understand why the big guy up in the sky has given me some of these talents, and I think the main reason is to help people.

TIGER PAUSE

Woods is the only player to win three consecutive U.S. Amateurs (1994-96).

PEOPLE ARE TALKING ABOUT TWO TYPES OF GOLFERS: TIGER WOODS AND EVERYBODY ELSE.[62]

—*NBC News Report*

HE'S GOD'S GIFT TO THE GAME, THAT'S ALL.[63]

—*Charlie Sifford, veteran golfer, an African-American*

I let my clubs do the talking. . . . But I'll tell you
this: I'm going to try to
get better. When I'm
sixty, maybe I'll look back
and see when my peak
was and how long my
prime lasted.

A beaming Woods celebrates his third consecutive U.S. Amateur victory, earned in 1996 when he beat Steve Scott on the first extra hole. (USGA photo)

TIGER HAS NOW JOINED MUHAMMAD ALI AND MICHAEL JOR-
DAN AS THE ATHLETES OF THE TV GENERATION WHO TRAN-
SCEND THEIR SPORTS IN TERMS OF ATTRACTING CASUAL (TEL-
EVISION) VIEWERS. IF TIGER IS ON, PEOPLE WANT TO WATCH
HIM, NO MATTER HOW FAR HE'S AHEAD.[64]

—Dick Ebersol, network television executive

These kids may not play golf. They may not be what I
am in a golfing sense. But they could be what I am in
a business field or a medical field.[65]

—regarding kids attending an inner-city golf clinic

No. I feel I have an obligation to serve as a role model
to everyone, regardless of color.

*—at the 1995 Masters, when asked if he had an
obligation to serve as a role model to minority youths*

WE'RE ALL LOOKING FOR ONE SCORE ALL THE TIME, AND IT'S HIS.

—*Colin Montgomerie*

My biggest goal, other than winning tournaments, is to make golf look like America. We're the melting pot of the world, all races and religions. I've grown through golf, and I want to have a positive impact on kids. I want every child in America to have the opportunity I had.[66]

When I talk to kids at the golf clinics I give, I'm not trying to preach to them that this is "a sport for you." I'm saying, "This is an opportunity for you to grow as a person." I think that is what really matters.[67]

Everything that I've learned in this game I've basically learned from somebody else. They've given me that knowledge, and it's my responsibility to pass that on and share that knowledge.

～

I think my emergence in golf, my ethnic background, has obviously been good for the game. It's gotten more minorities involved in the game. I think that's only going to be good for the game.

～

HE HAS RAISED THE BAR HIGHER THAN ANYBODY HAS EVER RAISED IT AS FAR AS BETWEEN HIM AND THE REST OF THE FIELD. HE SEEMS LIKE HE IS THE ONLY KID THAT CAN JUMP OVER IT RIGHT NOW.

—*Tom Watson*

～

Whether I win a lot of tournaments or not, I think my mark will probably be the kids that have followed.

I'm in a very unique position where a lot of kids look up to me just because I'm around their age group. And I think if I can influence their lives in a positive way, then I believe that's what the big guy in the sky had intended for me.

—during the 1997 Masters

Hopefully, kids will say a lot of positive things about me, and whether they want to strive to be me, or be better than me . . . that's great because then I know I have impacted their lives in a positive way.

TIGER PAUSE

In winning the 2000 Vardon Trophy for lowest scoring average on the PGA Tour, Woods finished 1.46 strokes ahead of second-place finisher Phil Mickelson. After Mickelson, another 1.46 strokes included the next forty-two places.

I don't think you ever want to become the next Tiger Woods or the next Jack Nicklaus or the next Michael Jordan or whatever. Try to be the best you can be. The things I have accomplished, other players accomplished, you can do that. Don't try to be like us: Try to be the best yourself you can be.

I BELIEVE THAT HE IS THE BEST GOLFER UNDER THE AGE OF THIRTY THAT THERE EVER HAS BEEN. I BELIEVE THAT HE IS GOING TO BE THE BEST GOLFER OF ANY AGE THAT THERE EVER HAS BEEN. I BELIEVE THAT HE IS GOING TO WIN MORE TOURNAMENTS THAN JACK NICKLAUS WON. I BELIEVE THAT HE IS GOING TO WIN MORE MAJOR CHAMPIONSHIPS THAN JACK NICKLAUS WON, AND I BELIEVE THAT BOTH OF THESE RECORDS ARE GOING TO STAND FOR TIGER WOODS LONGER THAN THEY HAVE STOOD FOR JACK NICKLAUS. I BELIEVE HE IS GOING TO BE RICH AND FAMOUS, AND I BELIEVE THAT HE IS GOING TO BRING GREAT JOY TO A HUGE NUMBER OF PEOPLE BECAUSE OF HIS ENORMOUS TALENT ON THE GOLF COURSE.[68]

—*Charles P. Pierce, writing in* GQ *magazine*

It's not too often you actually get a chance to influence a lot of people in a good way, and if you have that opportunity I think you should take it.[69]

I think I've attracted minorities to the game, but . . .
why limit it to just that? I think you should be able
to influence people in general, not just one race or
social economic (sic) background. Everybody should
be in the fold.[70]

I WASN'T ALIVE TO SEE MONET PAINT, BUT I AM ALIVE TO SEE
TIGER PLAY GOLF, AND THAT'S PRETTY GREAT.[71]

—*Phil Knight, Nike cofounder*

TIGERMANIA IS HEALTHY FOR GOLF. I DON'T THINK THERE'S
RESENTMENT OVER TIGER. IT'S A FASCINATION.[72]

—*D. A. Weibring, PGA Tour golfer*

INTIMIDATION

As far as intimidating other players, I just try to put myself in contention each and every time I go out. If they fall by the wayside because I'm there, so be it.

◠

I just go out and play. If someone wants to say that I'm the favorite, then so be it. The underdog, then so be it. I just focus on what I need to do. To be honest with you, I don't read what's written; I don't watch TV.

◠

THESE ARE THE BEST GOLFERS OF THE WORLD, PLAYING IN THE MOST PRESTIGIOUS TOURNAMENT IN THE WORLD, AND HE MADE IT LOOK LIKE A MONDAY OUTING WITH A BUNCH OF WEEKEND HACKERS.[73]

—*John Feinstein*

◠

Tiger Woods. [74]

—answer given by golfer Stuart Appleby, when asked at a
tournament what he had to shoot in order to win

MEDIA ATTENTION

There were photographers taking pictures of me who had never been on a golf course before. I went into my backswing and it sounded like rapid fire. I asked this one guy, "What are you doing?" He said something to me in German. I still don't know what he said.[75]

The problem can be solved very easily. In the States we have a one-arm-length rule—one away from the ropes. Here it's a little bit different. They walk in the middle of the fairways and stand right in front of you.
—*German Open press conference, May 2000*

If they're not talking to you, you're doing something wrong.

I played a practice round about 5:30 one morning and no one was out there. That was really nice.[76]

⌒

I guess the only time (the gallery) actually increased in size was probably Wednesday, when we were out here playing at 6:42 in the morning; a few hundred people out here. I definitely wouldn't get out that early to watch me play.

—at the 2000 Buick Invitational

⌒

There isn't enough time in the day or in my life to please everybody.[77]

⌒

I wish people could respect the fact that the golf course is our office, and we're trying to make a living. I wouldn't come into some guy's office while he's in a serious negotiation and say, "Excuse me, I hate to bother you, but could I get a picture?"[78]

⌒

Why would you want to talk to a guy who is nine shots out of the lead?

—*U.S. Open press conference, June 1997*

One thing that I wouldn't necessarily say I'm proud of, but I lead the Tour right now with *National Enquirer* covers.

Blowing my nose is not exactly an event.

The number of people—I've come to grips with that. That's not a problem. I actually kind of enjoy (when) a lot of kids come out, which is kind of neat. One thing I don't enjoy is how aggressive they are.

I take (media) shots for everything I do.[79]

⁓

People have something to gain off of me instead of just being a good friend.

⁓

I'm walking down the fairway and you hear a fan yell, "Can I have your autograph?" or, "Come take a picture with me." Would you say that to (Michael Jordan) on a fast break?

⁓

It's neat when kids are coming up to you and asking for autographs. It's bad when adults are running over the kids for autographs.

⁓

TIGER PAUSE

Upon turning professional, Woods signed his first endorsement deals with Nike and Titleist worth an estimated $60 million over five years. Later he signed an endorsement contract with Buick worth an estimated $30 million.

It's a lot easier to come to tournaments and not have to do a mandatory press conference every day. . . . You know, people still recognize me just the same.

I have gone out in Southern California. Granted, they are used to seeing Hollywood stars, so it is no big deal. In Orlando, it is a little different . . . They are not used to seeing people who are on TV. It is not a normal sight . . . That is what I find, the smaller cities I go to, people will react with more enthusiasm and lose it just a little bit more. Whereas, I think the greatest city in the world is New York because they don't care about anybody.

We played the first nine holes with about ten people around. You know that's never the case in the States. Unless I go off at dawn-thirty.

—at the 1999 American Express
Championship at Valderrama in Spain

MONEY

More than you.[80]

> —in response to a girl in New Orleans who
> asked him how much money he makes

I want to keep track of my money so they won't steal from me like ("they" did) Kareem Abdul-Jabbar.[81]

> —spoken at age fifteen when he first broached to
> his dad the subject of outside financial management

I'm not against it.

*—when asked his thoughts about increasing amounts of money
available in professional golf*

PGA TOUR

When guys on Tour sit around to have lunch and they are talking about . . . the draft in Vietnam, all that stuff, I was just born. . . . Now Sergio (Garcia) and I are talking about video games and what cartoons we watch.

⌒

DOES HE GET PREFERENTIAL TREATMENT? NO QUESTION. IF TIGER WANTS HOT AND COLD RUNNING BEER IN HIS HOUSE, ANYBODY WOULD ARRANGE IT TO GET HIM TO PLAY IN THEIR TOURNAMENT.[82]
—*Buddy Martin, media director of the International*

⌒

Golf courses are shortening up because of the fact that we are getting longer. Equipment's getting better; golfers are becoming athletes. And they're going to have to start making golf courses like the PGA (Championship) here, seventy-four hundred yards. And that's going to be the norm for a while until you get another crop of players that hit it by me thirty yards and make the course longer again.

TIGER IS DOMINANT AT EVERYTHING. PEOPLE MENTION BRAD FAXON OR JIM FURYK WHEN THEY TALK ABOUT THE BEST PUTTER ON TOUR. TIGER IS AS GOOD OR BETTER THAN THEY ARE. GUYS MENTION JUSTIN LEONARD AS THE BEST CHIPPER. TIGER IS A BETTER CHIPPER. PEOPLE TALK ABOUT DAVID DUVAL AND GREG NORMAN DRIVING THE BALL LONG AND STRAIGHT. TIGER IS LONGER AND STRAIGHTER. HE IS OVER-WHELMING THE GAME RIGHT NOW.[83]

—Paul Goydos, PGA Tour golfer

The only time he talks to me is when he wants me to do something for him, to play in this tournament or that tournament. It's not like he comes up to me and asks me how I'm doing.[84]

—*about his relationship with PGA Tour commissioner Tim Finchem*

THERE WAS RESISTANCE TO HIM ON THE TOUR AT FIRST BECAUSE HE HAD COME SO FAR SO YOUNG. BUT WHAT OVERCAME THAT WAS TIGER'S MANIFEST HUNGER TO COMPETE. IT IS NOT ARTIFICIAL. IT IS NOT FEIGNED. IT IS REAL AND GENUINE AND VERY FORMIDABLE.[85]

—*Charles P. Pierce, writing in* GQ *magazine*

POSITIVE THINKING

In my life, I've never gone to a tournament without thinking I could win . . . That's just the mind-set I have. Each and every tournament, I go there to try and win, something I've always believed in and I always will.

Don't give them any hope.
>   —*about his strategy at the 2000 U.S. Open,*
>   *which he eventually won by fifteen shots*

I WOULDN'T WANT TO SPEND THE NEXT TWENTY YEARS TRYING TO BEAT HIM. I TAKE THAT BACK. OF COURSE I WOULD.[86]

>   —*Jack Nicklaus*

I don't know what competitor likes finishing second. I don't understand why people are satisfied with that because that's not the ultimate goal. At least that's not mine. My ultimate goal is to win. And anything short of that I'm always going to be disappointed.

I believe in what I can do with a golf ball.[87]

I gained confidence at every level in all the tournaments I played. It teaches you something every time you win.

I've always felt I've been pretty tough mentally. I've felt that I've always had a mental edge over a lot of my opponents. . . . I always felt I could play to win. My mind won me a lot of tournaments.

You learn from your mistakes. You work on your thought process over a shot, what you could have done better. Or even if you executed a good one, what did you do right?

—about his mental approach to the game

Sometimes I pull it off and other times I don't, but if you want to win, you gotta go.[88]

I would every week.[89]

—when asked in Great Britain, where wagering on golf is both legal and popular, whether he would be inclined to wager on himself

If I play my normal game, I should be able to win. I think my game is good enough that I can do that. I think the biggest thing is to have the mind-set and the belief that you can win every tournament going in. That's where a lot of guys have their faults . . . So it's nice to win a tournament with your mind because that's what wins majors.[90]

I've never given up in my entire life on a golf course. And I'm very proud of that . . . You start going bad, who cares? You've got to get it back. You've got to hang in there and fight and claw and scratch and do whatever it takes.

TIGER PAUSE

Woods in one multiyear stretch won nineteen straight tournaments in which he shared or owned the fifty-four-hole lead.

~

Knowing that you never arrive is a wonderful thing because you never say, "This is my limit." You never put a limitation on your own abilities. I think that's where a lot of players, a lot of athletes in general, put limitations: "That's as good as I can play." I hear that all the time. . . . If you put a limitation on it, then you can't get any better.

~

I'll try any shot if it is the correct shot to play.

~

Woods blasts out of a bunker in the final round of the 1999 U.S. Open, which was won by the ill-fated Payne Stewart. (USGA photo by J. D. Cuban)

I believe in every shot I
hit that I can pull it off.
It's just, I guess, my
mind-set. I've always
believed that.

~

PRACTICE AND PREPARATION

AS FAR AS HE HITS IT, THERE'S NO REASON FOR HIM
TO EVER BOTHER TO PRACTICE HIS SHORT GAME.
—*Jack Nicklaus*

When I'm at home I'm trying to pick sides of the fairway I want to hit the ball on, shape it into ten-yard-wide fairways out there, that kind of thing, and I was able to do it. That leads you to believe that if you can do it there, you can definitely do it in a tournament.[91]

Probably my right thumb on the remote.[92]
    —*answer to query on what he would work on after a round*

I'LL NEVER FORGET THE DAY HE CAME TO ME WHEN
HE WAS STILL A LITTLE KID AND SAID, "HOW DO
YOU GET RID OF BACKSPIN?" I SAID, "TIGER, 99
PERCENT OF GOLFERS ARE DYING TO GET BACKSPIN,
NOT GET RID OF IT. WHY DON'T YOU KEEP THE SPIN
AND PLAY THE BALL PAST THE HOLE AND BRING IT
BACK?" HE JUST NODDED HIS HEAD. I COULD TELL
HE FILED THAT AWAY FOR FUTURE REFERENCE.[93]
                                    —*John Anselmo, early Woods mentor*

People have no idea how many hours I put into this game.[94]

TIGER PAUSE

By the age of six Woods was already listening
to subliminal motivational tapes.

⌒

Swing changes take time. If you start forcing it, you
are probably going to end up making mistakes and go
down the wrong path.

⌒

They have to be straight uphill putts. The smoother
and slower the greens, the quicker you'll make an
imprint on the green. After about twenty balls, you'll
see a light patch going toward the hole. Now you're
making the grain go that way. You just get up there
and hit it. I do one hundred, sometimes two hundred.
It's not that hard.[95]

*—about a common practice drill of making
two hundred six-foot putts . . . one-handed*

⌒

Throughout my junior golf, collegiate golf, and amateur golf days, there's always been one tournament per
year. That's it. It's either the Junior World when I was
real young, then the U.S. Junior, and then it became
the U.S. Amateur. Nothing else really mattered. There
was no other tournament that really came close, those
were the big ones to win. Now there are four of them
out here. You have to peak four different times.

    —on the difference between amateur and professional golf

Hard work. I practiced quite a bit as a kid. I always
kept it fun. I always liked to challenge myself or my
dad. Just trying to improve that through competition,
not necessarily by just going out there and beating
balls all day; that gets boring. I like to play games, play
situational games. . . . That's what every kid does. I did
the same thing in golf.

PRESSURE

I love feeling the pressure. I love it. I was telling my dad . . . "There's no better position than being up front."[96]

You have to love everybody chasing you and having all the pressure on you. . . . Michael Jordan, would he rather have the lead and have the ball in his hands with the chance to win or come from behind and do it that way? You'd always rather have the lead . . . I love that feeling of having everybody come after me. Give me your best shot. And if I can fend them off, great, and if I can't, I learn from it.

I WOULDN'T HAVE BEEN HAPPY UNTIL I HAD HIM TEN (DOWN) OR SOMETHING. HE'S THAT TOUGH.

—*Steve Scott, who lost to Woods in the U.S. Amateur final after being 5 up*

It's really interesting when you are coming down the stretch in a tournament and everything is on the line at that moment, (and) you forget what you have done. You forget how bad you have played or how good you have played. What really counts is the moment. It's right now. And that's what you focus on.

It is amazing what happens when you are pushed to the limit, emotionally, physically, and just a lot of different things are tested. And you find out a lot about yourself, what you have inside, in order to play at this level like this.[97]

I get nervous with every
shot. That's just
because I care.

I'm always nervous. The day I'm not is the day I quit. That means I don't care.[98]

⌒

I DON'T THINK I'D WANT TO TRADE PLACES WITH TIGER WOODS, TO BE HONEST.[99]

—*Mark O'Meara, 1998 Masters and British Open winner and Woods's good buddy*

⌒

If you don't like that pressure, you shouldn't be out there.

⌒

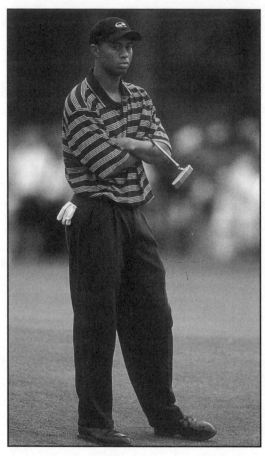

Not every moment in the life of a champion golfer is full of sunshine and roses. (USGA photo by John Mummert)

The most nervous I've ever been was probably that first tee at Augusta in '97, the final round. After what, unfortunately, happened to Greg (Norman) the last year, that was kind of on my mind, the fact that it can happen. Somebody can shoot a great round and I can blow it and I can lose the tournament with a nine-shot lead. And thinking about that on my first tee was definitely pretty daunting. But after I just ripped it right down the middle and hit a little wedge on the green, I was pretty relaxed after that.

TIGER PAUSE

Woods is one of three players (Jack Nicklaus and Phil Mickelson are the others) to win the individual title at the NCAA Championship and the U.S. Amateur in the same year.

It comes down to one thing: I've still got to hit the shot. Me. Alone. That's what I must never forget.[100]

That's what I love the most, doing it when it means the most.[101]

I like the feeling of trying my hardest under pressure. It's so intense sometimes, it's hard to breathe. It feels like a lion is tearing at my heart.[102]

That gives you confidence down the stretch, when you are a little nervous, hands are sweating, eyeballs are bugging. You can summon enough strength to do it again because you've done it before.

⌒

I love playing in the most intense pressure. How can you not? This is what we play for. This is why you play hard, why you practice, is to get in these positions where you have to be so committed to a shot and be so mentally exact that it takes a lot of effort.

⌒

It's always nice to play with all the pressure on the line. If you don't like that and you don't have fun doing that, then I don't know why you're even out there.

⌒

I'm not immune to feeling nerves and pressure. I don't think anyone is, if you really care about something.

PROFESSIONAL MAJORS

We all knew that if there were any two tournaments to win the Grand Slam on, it would be these two venues. It doesn't get any better than this, Pebble Beach and St. Andrews, and there's no better site to have it occur than the home of golf. That's where it all started.

—spoken during the 2000 U.S. Open at Pebble Beach, followed a month later by a trip to St. Andrew's for the British Open

I always have liked playing under tougher conditions. I don't like when you have to go out there and average 68 or 67 just to keep pace.

IF HE DOESN'T WIN THE BRITISH OPEN, THERE SHOULD BE A STEWARD'S INQUIRY.

—Michael Bonallack, captain and former secretary of the Royal and Ancient Golf Club at St. Andrews, during week of the 2000 U.S. Open at Pebble Beach

You would like to have your game peak at four different times a year, and that's something you always hope for and wish for and you plan for. To actually have it happen is a different story.

⌒

TIGER PAUSE

Woods completed his professional Grand Slam after having played in twenty-one majors. Of the other four players to have won the Masters, the United States and British Opens and the PGA Championship, Nicklaus did it in his twenty-seventh event, Gary Player his thirtieth, Ben Hogan his thirty-third, and Gene Sarazen his thirty-fifth.

⌒

A major championship is just a different type of animal than any other tournament.

⌒

I'm always disappointed when I don't win a major. . . . But, realistically, you're not going to win one every year you play. The greatest players that have ever played the game have never done that. All you can ask of yourself is to give yourself opportunities. There's four a year. If you can somehow have a chance to win on the back nine on Sunday on each and every one, I figure for the rest of my life I would have a few of them in my pocket.

I think the greatest record of all is eighteen professional majors (held by Jack Nicklaus).

TIGER PAUSE

Woods completed his professional Grand Slam at age twenty-four, two years earlier than the next youngest (Nicklaus).

I've always envisioned that I would have the Slam eventually. . . . But to beat some of the greatest champions this game has to offer and to play this great game of golf and to be able to win at this venue and to complete the Slam at this venue, that's what makes it so special.[103]

—on completing his career Grand Slam by virtue of winning the 2000 British Open at St. Andrews

I like to have my game peaking for those things.[104]

—talking about the four professional majors

SELF-EVALUATION

It was more like a C-plus.
—describing his last round when pressed to grade himself upon winning the 1997 GTE Byron Nelson Classic

People say that I look like I'm not having fun out there playing because I'm not smiling. Well, I'm focused; I'm trying to win. And you can't always smile when you're trying to win.

Well, I didn't really say encouraging words to myself walking off the green. I guess the word probably would be perturbed to the tenth power.
—at the 1999 PGA Championship, talking about his temper

(If) I'm in the lead with nine holes to go, I like my chances.

HE DIDN'T TRY TO DO ANYTHING THAT HE COULDN'T DO. I THOUGHT, THAT IS THE WAY YOU PLAY GOLF. THAT IS A GREAT LESSON FOR ME, OR FOR ANY GOLFER, TO PLAY WITHIN YOURSELF.

—Jack Nicklaus, at the 2000 PGA Championship

I played poorly all week. I felt pressure on every shot because I didn't know where the ball was going. The left trees were in play, the right trees were in play, the road was in play.[105]

—evaluating his performance at the 2000 Tour Championship after finishing eleven under par, two strokes behind the winner

U.S. OPEN

It's going to be a very difficult week. If you go around and make seventy-two straight pars, I guarantee you have a chance to win.

> *—prior to the 2000 U.S. Open, which he went on to win by fifteen shots at twelve under par*

To win our Open championship, to be an American, it's a great feeling. You think back on all the hard work you put into it, the times as a kid imagining you're trying to beat the best players in the world. To win it on Father's Day. I can't wait to give this [trophy] to my dad and let him rub it a little bit.

HE'S BEEN MORE DOMINATING OVER THIS PERIOD THAN I EVER WAS OVER ANY SIMILAR PERIOD OF TIME.

> *—Jack Nicklaus, during the 2000 U.S. Open at Pebble Beach*

I PLAYED ONE GOOD ROUND OF GOLF. BUT IF I PLAYED OUT OF MY MIND, I PROBABLY STILL WOULD HAVE LOST BY FIVE, SIX, OR SEVEN.

—*Ernie Els, 2000 U.S. Open*

The only thing I wanted to do today was, besides win the title, the thing I was grinding so hard not to do was not make a bogey. I wanted to go out there and play all eighteen holes in the final round of the U.S. Open with the lead with no bogeys.

—*2000 U.S. Open*

The other two majors were obviously great wins, but to win our Open Championship, being an American, I mean, it's a great feeling. It's hard to describe.

I've never had anything like this, even in fantasy golf.

—*on whether he ever envisioned leading the U.S. Open by ten strokes after three rounds*

WINNING (AND LOSING)

I love when people have to come get me. I love to feel that intensity, that fight. It's a great fight. And it's right where you want to be. Because you know that it's going to take more effort for them to come get you than it is for you to just maintain par.

Winning never gets old.[106]

TIGER WOODS MAKES PEOPLE THINK WINNING IS EASY.[107]

—*Ernie Els*

⌒

It's not easy, especially how deep the fields are now. I appreciate every victory I get.

⌒

It gives you great motivation, to lose. You can't win
everything. I guess I have always heard this the most
in the press: You always learn more by losing. I say yes
and no to that. Because there are times when I have
won, I have learned an awful lot.[108]

⌒

Winning is not always the barometer of improvement.

⌒

TIGER WOODS IS NOT BIGGER THAN THE GAME. THE OTHER
NIGHT I WAS LYING IN BED AND I SAID, "YOU KNOW WHAT?
I'M NOT PRAYING TO HIM. HE'S NOT A GOD. HE'S HUMAN
JUST LIKE I AM."[109]

*—Hal Sutton, PGA Tour golfer, who beat Woods
at the 2000 Players Championship*

⌒

TIGER PAUSE

In 2000 Woods became the first player ever to finish under par in every PGA Tour event he played.

A bomb could be going off, you probably wouldn't even know. That's the focus I had.

—about his narrow win over Sergio Garcia
at the 1999 PGA Championship

I welcome a challenge. That is why we play out here. I know that is why I play—to challenge myself and to hopefully come out on top against the best players. And to know that I have beaten the best, that makes it even sweeter.

It's not as important as people might think. I think the
most important factor is just winning tournaments.
The ranking will take care of itself if you just win.
There's no better feeling than winning tournaments.
        —*when asked about the importance of the No. 1 ranking*

I can tell you one thing, I am not against playing with
a big lead.

It's nice to win, but it feels a little bit better when you
can actually say that you beat the best.

The patented fist pump tells it all—Tiger Woods has just polished off his fifteen-stroke victory at the 2000 U.S. Open at Pebble Beach. (USGA photo by John Mummert)

I think you have to be more realistic in your expectations in winning golf tournaments at every level. I remember when I was eleven years old, I won thirty tournaments in a row. You can't do that out here. It won't happen. As you go up in levels, you win less and less and less, just because the fields are deeper, players are better.

I'm going to celebrate like hell tonight.

—in 1996, *after winning his third consecutive U.S. Amateur title*

WORK ETHIC

I understood exactly what he meant—that no one is going to give you anything in life unless you work hard and bust your rear end, and even then charity might not come your way. He helped establish my work ethic early, and for that I'll forever be grateful.[110]

—talking about his father, Earl

There's no substitute for hard work.

TIGER PAUSE

Woods holds the record for the largest margin of victory at the Masters (twelve strokes, 1997) and the U.S. Open (fifteen strokes, 2000). The twelve-shot win was the fourth-highest in PGA Tour history; his fifteen-shot win was the second best in history and the widest margin of victory on tour since 1948.

I've always felt that I've always had a mental edge over a lot of my opponents. It doesn't mean that I have the physical abilities to back it up, but I always felt that I could play with them mentally. I had the desire to win. I wanted to beat you.[111]

I will try as hard as I possibly can. Just like I do every round. That's a given. It's a constant.

I WOULD WATCH EVERYTHING TIGER DOES AND THEN DO
MORE. IN THE GYM, ON THE PRACTICE TEE, I'D MAKE A POINT
OF LEAVING AFTER HE DOES. WHATEVER MENTAL EXERCISES
HE DOES, DOUBLE THEM. THAT'S WHAT HOGAN DID, WHAT
TREVINO DID, WHAT I DID. DON'T LET ANYONE, EVEN TIGER,
OUTWORK YOU.[112]

*—Gary Player, discussing ways other Tour players
can challenge or beat Woods*

SON, YOU GET OUT OF IT WHAT YOU PUT INTO IT.[113]

—Earl Woods, quoting advice from his own father

I have always worked this hard. This is what I do. This is just me. . . But I think what it all boils down to is how bad do you really want it when you play. And, you can work out all you want, you can have the right diet, practice as hard as you want, but when it comes down the stretch in a tournament, all that is kind of thrown out the door. It is, How bad do you really want to win?

—*on whether his work ethic has inspired others to work harder*

TIGER PAUSE

When he won the 2000 British Open, Woods had simultaneously held or shared the record of being the most under par in each of the four professional majors: eighteen under par at the Masters, twelve under at the U.S. Open, nineteen under at the British Open, eighteen under at the PGA Championship.

Woods following through at the 1999 U.S. Open with perhaps the game's most powerful swing. (USGA photo by John Mummert)

I just love to compete. I don't care if it's golf or Nintendo or in the classroom. I mean, competing against the other students or competing against myself. I know what I'm capable of.[114]

Notes

1. *Sports Argus*, January 8, 2000.
2. *Ibid.*
3. Tim Rosaforte, *Tiger Woods: The Makings of a Champion*. New York: St. Martin's, 1997, p. 19.
4. *New York Times*, April 3, 2000.
5. *Washington Post*, June 19, 2000.
6. *Sports Illustrated*, September 4, 2000.
7. *Jet*, April 28, 1997.
8. *Golf Digest*, April 2000.
9. *Ibid.*
10. *Good Morning America*, ABC-TV, April 15, 1997.
11. *Los Angeles Times*, April 5, 2000.
12. *Larry King Live*, CNN, June 10, 1998.
13. Rosaforte, p. 120.
14. Rosaforte, p. 128.
15. *Sports Illustrated*, August 28, 2000.
16. *New York Times*, June 2000.

17. *Golf World*, September 1, 2000.
18. *Sports Illustrated*, November 13, 2000.
19. *Sports Illustrated*, September 4, 2000.
20. *Golf World*, September 15, 2000.
21. *Newsweek*, April 10, 1995.
22. *New York Times*, April 3, 2000.
23. *Sports Illustrated for Kids*, June 1998.
24. *Golf Digest*, January 2000.
25. Rosaforte, p. 129.
26. *Jet*, May 26, 1997.
27. *Sports Illustrated*, May 26, 1997.
28. Rosaforte, p. 63.
29. *USA Today*, September 14, 1994.
30. *Newsweek*, April 28, 1997.
31. Rosaforte, p. 22.
32. Ibid., p. 5.
33. Ibid., p. 253.
34. Ibid., p. 185.
35. Ibid., p. 233.
36. Earl Woods with Pete McDaniel, *Training a Tiger, A Father's Guide to Raising a Winner in Both Golf and Life*. New York: HarperCollins, 1997.
37. *Sports Illustrated for Kids*, June 1998.
38. *Parks and Recreation*, January 1998.
39. National Public Radio, June 18, 1998.
40. *People Magazine*, July 24, 2000.
41. *Gentlemen's Quarterly*, April 1997.
42. Rosaforte, p. 159.
43. NBC News, April 13, 1997.

44. *Daily News Record*, April 27, 2000.
45. National Public Radio, April 14, 1997.
46. *Sports Illustrated*, September 4, 2000.
47. Rosaforte, p. 24.
48. *Sports Illustrated*, April 13, 1998.
49. *Golf Magazine*, April 1998.
50. *Sports Illustrated*, March 8, 1999.
51. *Larry King Live*, CNN, June 10, 1998.
52. *Larry King Live*, CNN, June 10, 1998.
53. *Larry King Live*, CNN, June 10, 1998.
54. *Black Enterprise*, September 1997.
55. *Fortune*, May 12, 1997.
56. *Newsweek*, April 28, 1997.
57. Rosaforte, p. 32.
58. *Sports Illustrated*, December 8, 1997.
59. *Las Vegas Review-Journal*, October 8, 2000.
60. NBC News, April 14, 1997.
61. *Jet* , June 21, 1999.
62. NBC News, April 14, 1997.
63. NBC News, April 13, 1997.
64. *Washington Post*, June 20, 2000.
65. Associated Press, June 2000.
66. *Golf Digest*, April 2000.
67. *Sport Magazine*, October 1997.
68. *Gentlemen's Quarterly*, April 1997.
69. *Larry King Live*, CNN, June 10, 1998.
70. *Larry King Live*, CNN, June 10, 1998.
71. Rosaforte, p. 165.
72. Ibid., p. 187.

73. National Public Radio, April 14, 1997.

74. *Sports Illustrated*, August 28, 2000.

75. *New York Times*, June 7, 2000.

76. *Sports Illustrated*, September 4, 2000.

77. *Time*, August 14, 2000.

78. *Sports Illustrated*, May 19, 1997.

79. *Larry King Live*, CNN, June 10, 1998.

80. *Time*, August 14, 2000.

81. Rosaforte, p. 45.

82. *Sports Illustrated*, April 3, 2000.

83. *Sports Illustrated*, June 5, 2000.

84. *Golf World*, November 10, 2000.

85. *Gentlemen's Quarterly*, April 1997.

86. *Sports Illustrated*, August 28, 2000.

87. CNN, July 20, 2000.

88. *Larry King Live*, CNN, June 10, 1998.

89. CNN, July 20, 2000.

90. *Sports Illustrated*, July 14, 1997.

91. *Washington Post*, June 14, 2000.

92. *Washington Post*, May 12, 2000.

93. *Sports Illustrated*, April 3, 2000.

94. Associated Press, June 2000.

95. *Golf Digest*, April 2000.

96. Associated Press, July 5, 1999.

97. CNN, August 21, 2000.

98. *Sports Illustrated*, May 18, 1998.

99. Rosaforte, p. 255.

100. *Sports Illustrated*, January 20, 1997.

101. *Sports Illustrated*, April 7, 1997.

102. Rosaforte.
103. CNN, July 23, 2000.
104. *Larry King Live*, CNN, June 10, 1998.
105. *Sports Illustrated*, November 13, 2000.
106. *Barbara Walters Presents*, ABC-TV, December 2, 1997.
107. *Sports Illustrated*, April 24, 2000.
108. CNN, April 6, 2000.
109. *Sports Illustrated*, April 3, 2000.
110. *Jet*, June 16, 1997.
111. CNN, June 14, 2000.
112. *Sports Illustrated*, November 13, 2000.
113. Woods and McDaniel.
114. *Gentlemen's Quarterly*, April 1997.